WANTING TO BELIEVE
BIBLE STUDY
FAITH, FAMILY, AND FINDING AN EXCEPTIONAL LIFE

RYAN DOBSON

developed with Nic Allen and
Elizabeth Hyndman

LifeWay Press®
Nashville, Tennessee

Published by LifeWay Press®
© 2014 Siggie, LLC

Wanting to Believe © 2014 by Ryan Dobson. Published by B&H Publishing Group; Nashville, TN. Used by Permission.

No part of this book may be reproduced or transmitted in any form or by any means, electronic or mechanical, including photocopying and recording, or by any information storage or retrieval system, except as may be expressly permitted in writing by the publisher. Requests for permission should be addressed in writing to LifeWay Press®; One LifeWay Plaza; Nashville, TN 37234-0152.

ISBN: 978-1-4300-3298-4
Item: 005650410

Dewey decimal classification: 234.2
Subject headings: FAITH \ BELIEF AND DOUBT \ CHRISTIAN LIFE

Unless indicated otherwise, all Scripture quotations are taken from the Holman Christian Standard Bible. Copyright © 1999, 2000, 2002, 2003, 2009 by Holman Bible Publishers. Used by permission. Holman Christian Standard Bible® and HCSB® are federally registered trademarks of Holman Bible Publishers.

To order additional copies of this resource, write to LifeWay Church Resources, Customer Service, One LifeWay Plaza, Nashville, TN 37234-0113; fax 615.251.5933; phone 800.458.2772; order online at *www.lifeway.com* or email *orderentry@lifeway.com;* or visit the LifeWay Christian Store serving you.

Printed in the United States of America

Adult Ministry Publishing, LifeWay Church Resources, One LifeWay Plaza, Nashville, TN 37234-0152

Contents

About the Author 4

How to Use This Study 5

Guidelines for Groups 6

Introduction 7

WEEK 1
Believe 9

WEEK 2
Fascination, Not Frustration 21

WEEK 3
Whatever It Takes 33

WEEK 4
Remember the Individual 45

Key Insights 57

Leader Notes 58

Further Resources 60

Introducing Your Child to Christ 61

About the Author

RYAN DOBSON grew up in the spotlight as the son of America's foremost family expert, author, and radio broadcaster, Dr. James Dobson. While some would be tempted to wilt under these circumstances, Ryan trusted the Lord to guide him.

Ryan's first book, *Be Intolerant,* was followed up with five more books, and then, along with the eight-part *Building a Family Legacy* series with Dr. James Dobson, *Wanting to Believe.* In 2006, Ryan launched his own broadcast with the purpose of "building passion and identity in Christ followers." Then in 2010, Ryan joined forces with his dad as co-host of *Dr. James Dobson's Family Talk* and currently serves as VP of Broadcast. Ryan continues to travel sharing the gospel of Jesus Christ, defending life, and giving much needed encouragement and advice to couples and parents.

Ryan lives in Colorado with his wife and two children, Lincoln Cash and Luci Rose.

NIC ALLEN helped with the curriculum development of this study. After spending ten years in student ministry, Nic became the family and children's pastor at Rolling Hills Community Church in Franklin, Tennessee. Nic has written for several LifeWay Bible studies, including *Courageous, Facing the Giants,* and *Flywheel.* Nic and his wife, Susan, have three children: Lillie Cate, Nora Blake, and Simon.

ELIZABETH HYNDMAN also helped develop this study. Elizabeth holds a Master of Arts in Biblical Counseling from Southern Baptist Theological Seminary and serves as an editor at LifeWay Christian Resources.

How to Use This Study

The four sessions of this study may be used weekly or during a weekend retreat. But we recommend that before you dig into this material, you watch the film, *Wanting to Believe* by Ryan Dobson from the *Dr. James Dobson Presents: Building a Family Legacy* film series. This will lay the groundwork for your study.

This material has been written for a small-group experience, for you and your spouse, or for personal study.

An option to extend or conclude this study is for your group to view the film *Your Legacy* from the *Dr. James Dobson Presents: Building a Family Legacy* film series.

CONNECT: The purpose of the introductory section of each session invites and motivates you to connect with the topic of the session and others in your group.

WATCH: The study DVD contains four videos which include clips from a talk by Ryan Dobson based on the film and the accompanying book *Wanting to Believe* by Ryan Dobson (B&H Publishing Group, ISBN 978-1-4336-8252-0).

ENGAGE: This section is the primary focus of each week's group time. You and the other participants will further engage the truths of Scripture and discuss accompanying questions. This section will also include a Wrap Up portion, which concludes the group session and leads to the Reflect section.

REFLECT: This at-home study section helps you dig deeper into Scripture and apply the truths you're learning. Go deeper each week by reading the suggested chapters in the book *Wanting to Believe* and completing the activities at the end of each session in this study.

Guidelines for Groups

While you can complete this study alone, you will benefit greatly from covering the material with the interaction of a Sunday school class or small group. Here are a few ways to cultivate a valuable experience as you engage in this study.

PREPARATION: To get the most out of each group time, read through the study each week and answer the questions so you're ready to discuss the material. It will also be helpful for you and your group members to have copies of the book *Wanting to Believe* (ISBN 978-1-4336-8252-0). Read it in advance of the study to prepare, and encourage your members to read the corresponding chapters each week. In your group, don't let one or two people shoulder the entire responsibility for conversation and participation. Everyone can pitch in and contribute.

CONFIDENTIALITY: In the study, you will be prompted to share thoughts, feelings, and personal experiences. Accept others where they are without judgment. Many of the challenges discussed will be private. These should be kept in strict confidence by the group.

RESPECT: Participants must respect each other's thoughts and opinions, providing a safe place for those insights to be shared without fear of judgment or unsolicited advice (including hints, sermons, instructions, and scriptural Band-Aids®). Take off your fix-it hat and leave it at the door, so you can just listen. If advice is requested, then it's okay to lend your opinion, seasoned with grace and offered with love.

ACCOUNTABILITY: Each week, participants will be challenged to live out their beliefs. Commit to supporting and encouraging each other during the sessions and praying for each other between meetings.

Introduction

In Mark 9, there's a story of Jesus healing a boy possessed with a demon. What I find intriguing about this story is not the healing, though that is amazing. What I love about this story is the transparency of the boy's father. He asks Jesus to heal his son, *if He can*. Jesus replies, "'If You can?' Everything is possible to the one who believes."

And this is my favorite part—the father answers Jesus, "I do believe! Help my unbelief."

I feel so often that my prayers to God are similar—I do believe! Help my unbelief. My faith journey could be summed up in those six words. Based on my experience teaching and talking with others, I know that many of you pray that prayer, too.

I spend a lot of time speaking to groups of people about God—His character, His power, His presence in our lives, and what it means to follow Him. After each talk, I invite people to talk with me. Over and over, I have people tell me they *want to believe*. They want to believe what I'm saying is true.

My advice to all of them—my advice to myself—is to choose to believe. Belief is a choice.

Even after we become Christ followers, we must continually choose to believe in the promises of God and His character, though we may not always feel like they are true. Along with making the choice to believe, we make the choice every day to live like what we believe is true. If we believe the character of God, His power and presence in our lives, we will want to follow Him. Following God requires more choices. We must daily choose to believe, to love our spouses, to love our children, and to love others.

I had a front row seat to a great example of someone who constantly chose to believe and act on those beliefs. I've made some spectacularly bad choices throughout my life, but if there is one reason I kept coming back to truth, that reason is my dad.

Dr. James C. Dobson spent the entirety of his professional life speaking the truth. But he didn't stop at his professional life. Dr. Dobson, my dad, chose daily to believe and love. The truths he teaches and his choice to live them out have formed the structure of my own life, as well as the structure of this Bible study.

My hope is that by doing this study, you will pray, "I do believe! Help my unbelief." I hope you will choose to believe and that you will choose to love—your spouse, your children, and others.

WEEK 1
BELIEVE

CONNECT

● **BEFORE YOU BEGIN,** take time to pray with your group. Ask God to teach the group how to know and believe the truth found in His Word.

This study is about knowing what you believe and applying it to the way you love others. Get your group started by sharing a bit about your faith journeys. Use the questions below as a sort of outline to allow everyone time to talk and be heard.

> What was your life like before you chose to follow Christ?

> Describe the way you came to know Christ as your Savior and the Lord of your life.

> What were some immediate evidences of Jesus in your life?

> What is God teaching you now?

If you have not yet made the decision to believe in Jesus as your Savior and the Lord of your life, consider asking your group leader for more information about becoming a follower of Christ. Perhaps this study and the stories and experiences of the others in your group will help answer questions and concerns you may have.

Wanting to Believe

WATCH

● **WATCH CLIP 1** from the study DVD and answer the following questions:

In the clip, I talked about God getting my attention one night on an RV trip. He was talking to me about priorities and plans. Ultimately, He was asking me to live out what I believe.

What's important to you?

Take the things you listed as important, and write out some goals for each one.

What's Important   Goals

....

....

....

What are you doing each day to achieve the goals you listed?

Tell your spouse and/or your children your plans to meet your goals.

One way of defining what's important to us is to look at what we believe. This entire study is about taking what we believe and setting goals to live out those beliefs in our marriage, with our children, and through our relationships with those around us.

Believe

ENGAGE

● **CONTINUE YOUR GROUP TIME** with this discussion guide.

The title of this study is "Wanting to Believe," because sometimes the wanting comes before the belief. Sometimes we struggle to know and believe the truths we have heard about God and what He can do in our lives.

● **READ** Mark 9:14-27.

> Have you ever felt like the father in this story, crying out, "I do believe! Help my unbelief."? What happened next for you?

> What happened for the father in this story?

> Jesus said that everything is possible for those who believe. Do you believe that? How does that affect the way you pray? The way you live?

The man in this true story from Scripture was caught between hearing truth and fully believing it. But he was willing to step out of the crowd and speak honestly. I love his statement, "I do believe!" immediately followed by the prayer for help in his unbelief. That is where I feel I am most of the time. I feel like I believe, but I want to *really* believe. I want to know.

● **READ** Colossians 1:15-23.

Before he gets fully into the letter to the Colossians, Paul stops to lay out what it is he believes. These verses tell the Colossians the basis of the rest of the letter. Paul is saying, "Because I believe this,

I am writing you. Because I believe this, I am telling you these things. Because I believe this, I believe the rest of this letter is true."

> **What do you believe? Take time to write out what you believe to be true about God, His Son, and your salvation. Use the verses from Colossians as a guide.**

● **READ** 1 John 4:13-16.

Read the first part of verse 16 again. Did you catch that? "We have come to know and to believe."

Beth Moore talks about this verse in the *Children of the Day* Bible study.

> We've come to know it and believe it. Listen, He's already done it. But you've got to do your part. ... There comes a time when you get into the Scriptures, you realize that you are called to faith. Do a study of the love of God. Do you know it? Do you know what form it takes in the Scriptures? Do you know all the many times you are told how loved you are? Have you seen the extreme to which He went to reveal to you His great love? What sacrifice He made so that you would be sure to know that you are greatly loved. ... At some point we've got to quit saying, "I just don't feel like He loves me." Let's own our unbelief because that's not His breakdown. That's our unbelief. Know and believe—know and believe—know and believe.[1]

> **Do you think there's a difference between knowing and believing? What is the difference?**

Believe

Are there any attributes of God that you find difficult to know and believe? Why do you think that is?

These verses contain a promise. We have assurance that whoever confesses Christ remains in God and God in Him. Even when we struggle to believe the promises of God, He is consistent. We remain in Him because His love abides in us.

● **READ** James 2:20-24.

What do you think it means when James says faith without works is dead?

Describe a time when you believed something to be true, but did not act on those beliefs.

Most of the time, when we believe something—truly believe—we act on it. If we believe a house is on fire, we'll get out of it! If we believe we'll get free ice cream for waiting in line, we wait in line. If we believe our kids will hurt themselves on a trampoline, we buy nets and pads.

When we truly believe God is who He says He is, we'll act on it. Our lives will look different than they did before we believed. Our marriages, our parenting, and the way we treat others will all be different.

THIS WEEK'S INSIGHTS
• • •

- Believing in God's promises takes faith. Sometimes we have to ask for help when we struggle with unbelief.
- It is important to know what we believe.
- Our beliefs will affect our behavior.

What in your life will change if you know and believe in God's promises?

WRAP UP
• • •

THIS WEEK, make this your prayer.

> Father, thank You for Your Word, which points me to who You are. Thank You for showing me how to believe in You. Thank You for loving me even when I struggle to believe. Please help my unbelief. Help me to align my life with what I believe to be true. Amen.

REFLECT

● **READ AND COMPLETE** the activities for this section before your next group time. For further insight, read chapters 1, 2, 5, and 16 in the book *Wanting to Believe*.

This study is, in part, about taking inventory. It's about evaluating the practices, attitudes, schedules, relationships, and priorities in your life. It is about eliminating waste and focusing on what really matters. It is about being able to look over the sum of your life and knowing you lived out what you believe.

STRONG FOUNDATION

● **READ** Matthew 7:24-28.

> What type of person does the man who built his house on the sand represent? The man who built his house on the rock?

The Bible calls us not only to know and believe, but also to act on those beliefs. Jesus taught His followers about listening to and obeying His words by using a story about building houses. He didn't talk about the type of home each man built or what materials each one used. The problem wasn't the floor plan. It was the foundation. Building anything on a faulty foundation is foolish.

> What kind of foundation is your life built on?

> How do your actions, attitudes, and relationships line up with your foundation? Give a few examples.

When the storms come, our foundation—the non-negotiable things we believe—is revealed. In my own life, the storms have raged many times. Each time, I come back to the truth, returning to add another layer to the foundation upon which my life has been built. I keep coming back to that foundation because of God's relentless pursuit of me and my dad's example of faith.

When the storm of infertility nearly knocked them over, my parents' foundation remained strong. They prayed and trusted God through it all. It is because of their trust in Him that I was adopted. My parents believed God had a special plan for them and for me, for our good.

● **READ** Romans 8:28-29.

> What does it mean for all things to work together "for the good" of those who follow God?

Verse 29 explains that good for those who follow God means being conformed to Him. Becoming more like Jesus is always good, but can sometimes be uncomfortable, even painful. It is often in these times more than any other that we must cry, "I do believe! Help my unbelief." We must rely on our faithful God, knowing He is in control.

> Recall a time when even a difficult season proved to be part of God's plan for your ultimate good.

Believe

REFLECT

TAKE INVENTORY

The first step to figuring out if your life reflects your foundation—what you know and believe—is to take inventory. This can help determine what you value and what goals you should set to grow in your beliefs and relationship with Christ.

> Ask yourself:
> How do I spend most of my time? (It may be helpful to pull out your calendar, or chart your activities for a week to get an accurate view.)
>
> How do I use my resources? (Bank statements can be very enlightening.)
>
> What would others see as most valuable to me? (Ask some close friends; ask your children. Their answers may surprise you!)

DO WHAT YOU BELIEVE

● **READ** James 1:22-24.

> According to these verses, what is the result when we only listen to God's Word and neglect obedience?

> Describe a time when you knew what to do but didn't follow through. What were the consequences? How did you learn from that experience?

When we hear but don't do, when we preach but don't practice, when we use our lips but not also our lives, we're like the amnesiac being described in these verses: we lose touch with the core of who we are. We forget our foundation.

> How can you prevent forgetfulness when it comes to your faith—your foundation?

To remember our foundation and to act on our beliefs, God's priorities must become our priorities. The desire of our hearts should be to develop goals that are rooted in His Word.

> Read the following verses and make a determination of what God thinks is important based on the text.
> ☐ James 1:27
> ☐ Micah 6:8
> ☐ Psalm 51:17
> ☐ John 4:23-24
> ☐ Exodus 20:4-6

> As you reflect on these verses, are there things from your inventory you need to reevaluate? What needs to take a back seat to other priorities in order to better honor God and live out what you believe?

REFLECT

When you identify spiritual goals as a Christ follower, the things in your life that honor God begin to take more prominence, while the things that do not begin to fade away.

These goals should accurately reflect your beliefs, and should exist to honor and please God. Your relationship with Him should completely govern your sights and your steps.

> **What are some goals you need to set in order to conform more to Christ—to help your life match your belief and foundation?**

PERSONAL REFLECTION
• • •

This week, spend some time in prayer, renewing your commitment to following Christ. Your foundation will not reflect a Savior you do not follow. You can only follow a God you know. You cannot live out a foundation you do not have.

> **What steps can you take this week toward your goals? What can you do today?**

---

1. Beth Moore, *Children of the Day*, DVD teaching session (Nashville: LifeWay Press, 2014).

WEEK 2
FASCINATION
NOT FRUSTRATION

CONNECT

● **START YOUR GROUP TIME** by discussing what participants discovered in their Reflect homework.

This week, we'll be talking about how to live out what we believe about God's truth in our marriages. Get to know the other couples in your group better with the questions below.

How did you meet your husband or wife?

What first drew you to him or her?

Describe the moment you knew you loved him or her?

What has surprised you most about your spouse over the years?

One of the keys to a strong, happy marriage is choosing to continually be fascinated by our spouse and the differences between us. We all have moments of frustration with our spouse. We'll learn this week how to turn those moments into fascination, instead.

Wanting to Believe

WATCH

- **WATCH CLIP 2** from the study DVD and answer the following questions:

    If someone were to look at your life, what would they say is important to you?

    How does your answer to the last question match up with last week's list of what's important to you?

For Christians who are married, next to God, the most important person in our lives should be our spouse. We want to prioritize that relationship above all others. Therefore, our goals should include making our marriage healthy, committing to our husband or wife, and growing together in Christ.

    What goals can you set with your spouse to prioritize your marriage? Be specific.

    What one thing can you do this week to let your spouse know that he or she is important to you?

This week, we will look more closely at how to prioritize our marriage and live out what we believe by being a good husband or wife.

Fascination Not Frustration

ENGAGE

● **CONTINUE YOUR GROUP TIME** with this discussion guide.

The way we love and treat our spouse speaks volumes about our beliefs—both to our children and to those around us. I have said that the greatest contribution my parents made to my life was having a happy marriage—a marriage just as strong today as it was over half a century ago. My parents lived out their beliefs in their marriage.

● **READ** John 13:34-35.

> How does Jesus predict the world will know the disciples are His?

> Think about a Christian couple you respect. What do you admire about them? What about the way they love each other points to Christ?

> Do you think people look at your own marriage and know what you believe? Why or why not?

This is one of the last commands Jesus gave His disciples. The world will know about Christ when they see how His followers love one another. Likewise, one of the best ways to show Christ to others is through a committed, happy marriage.

One of the ways my parents have kept their marriage healthy is by continually choosing fascination over frustration. As my dad puts it, in a happy marriage, "both partners relish the mystery of each other, instead of assuming they know all there is to know." This way, marriage is always new.

The Bible has many passages that show us how to keep our marriage new and how to choose fascination over frustration.

● **READ** 1 Corinthians 13:4-7.

This passage is probably a familiar one. Try to read it with fresh eyes.

> **How do these aspects of love apply to your marriage?**

> **Which of these do you find the easiest to implement? Which do you find the most difficult?**

> **Is there an aspect of love you find easy to live out with others, but more difficult with your spouse? Why do you think that is?**

With love, we always have a choice. We are as fascinated with our spouse as we choose to be. We can choose to be patient and kind, or we can choose to be boastful, envious, conceited, and selfish. We can choose to love or not to love. In marriage, we have a choice in moments when our spouse does something that surprises us. We can be fascinated by who they are, instead of frustrated by what they do.

> **Do you agree that love is a choice? Why or why not?**

Fascination Not Frustration

How have you seen choosing love lived out, in your own life, or in the life of someone you know?

● **READ** Colossians 3:12-17.

What does love look like, according to this passage?

Which of the actions Paul calls Christians to "put on" is most difficult for you? Which is easiest?

Which action does your spouse do well?

How can you "put on love" in your marriage? Be as specific as possible.

When we are called to "put on" something in Scripture, it is often done after we "put off" something else. (See Col. 3:5-10.) This is possible through Jesus and a new life in Him. In our marriages, we need to constantly put off frustration and put on fascination. We need to choose love over annoyance at every turn.

THIS WEEK'S INSIGHTS
• • •

- One of the best ways to live out our beliefs is through a happy and committed marriage.
- Love is a choice. Because of Jesus, we can choose to love at every opportunity.
- We must put off frustration and put on fascination when it comes to our spouses and our differences.

What is a practical way you can put on fascination with your spouse this week?

WRAP UP
• • •

THIS WEEK, make this your prayer as you continue to consider what it looks like to choose fascination over frustration.

> God, thank You for giving me the opportunity to grow with and love the spouse you've given me. Thank You for making them unique and multi-faceted. Please help me to consistently be fascinated with the person I'm married to. Help us to both grow closer to You as we choose to love one another daily. Amen.

REFLECT

• **READ AND COMPLETE** the activities for this section before your next group time. For further insight, read chapter 9 in the book *Wanting to Believe*.

WHO ARE YOU?

One of the things my dad taught me about marriage is to always make sure I'm asking my wife, "Who are *you*?" instead of "Who *are* you?" The difference is subtle, but it is huge in meaning. The first question implies fascination—who is this beautiful, unique image-bearer I am married to?—while the second implies frustration—I don't even feel like I know this person.

When our husband or wife surprises us—and they often will—we have the opportunity to react in fascination or frustration. The key to a happy marriage is to choose fascination each time.

> When in your marriage have you asked, "Who are *you?*" How does your spouse still surprise you?

> As you consider your relationship with your spouse, do you find yourself more easily fascinated or frustrated? Why do you think that is?

COVERING A MULTITUDE OF SIN

One of the keys of avoiding frustration with anyone, but especially our spouses, is to forgive.

- **READ** 1 Peter 4:8 and Proverbs 10:12.

    What does it look like when love covers offenses?

    How have you seen love cover a multitude of sins in your life?

    Does the love you have for your spouse lead you to forgiveness, covering a multitude of sin? How could you improve?

- **READ** Ephesians 4:31-32.

    What are we called to remove from our lives in these verses?

    In contrast, what do these verses tell us to be?

    What motivation are we given for forgiving one another?

When we remember that Christ's love covered the multitude of our sins, it becomes easier for us to forgive others. Forgiving our spouses for their wrongdoings—the things that frustrate us—is a small thing compared to our forgiveness in Christ.

MARRIAGE MAINTENANCE

Aside from simply telling me to choose fascination over frustration, I've watched my dad demonstrate this time and again. The ease and joy in which he and my mom have conversations is delightful to watch. I once saw them cheerfully recount a story in which they both had opportunities to be frustrated.

They had been traveling, and my dad accidentally spilled tomato juice on my mom's brand new white pantsuit. He, admittedly inappropriately, began to laugh. She poured the rest of the juice in his lap! I watched them tell this story and laugh. My mom kissed my dad on the cheek. They both chose fascination over frustration, love and forgiveness over annoyance and complaining.

> **What would happen if more couples chose to laugh together instead of allowing the little things to cause frustration in their marriages?**

My parents can choose fascination over frustration because they spend time maintaining their marriage. They try to please one another. It's something I've tried to practice in my own marriage. I know what my wife, Laura, likes and so I try to do those things as often as possible. For example, Laura loves to get cards and flowers from me. So, I put reminders in my calendar to buy her cards and flowers. It's a simple way for me to choose to love her.

> **What things does your spouse love? Make a list. Beside each item, write a time in the next month to do those things for him or her.**

My Husband/Wife Loves	Time

FOR THE LORD

● **READ** Colossians 3:23-24 and 1 Corinthians 10:31.

> From these passages, write your "mission statement" as a follower of Christ.

> What does it look like to live the goals laid out in these verses?

> What implications do these verses have for marriage?

As believers, we must orient everything we say and do around glorifying Christ. This includes our marriage. If our ultimate goal is to glorify God, then we will want to choose to love our spouses. If we love our spouses enthusiastically, as to the Lord, even when they surprise us, the world will recognize our love for that which comes through God.

> How does loving your spouse enthusiastically differ from the norm? How does it differ from the way you love your spouse now?

Fascination Not Frustration

REFLECT

What steps can you take this week to love your spouse more enthusiastically and as the Lord would desire?

Our ultimate goal is to love God and bring Him glory. We do that by loving our husband or wife. We do that by having a happy, committed marriage. We do that by choosing fascination over frustration.

PERSONAL REFLECTION
• • •

This week, ask God to help you see the ways He has and continues to forgive you. Ask Him to help you forgive your spouse in the same way. Ask Him to help you put on kindness and compassion and ask of your spouse, "Who are *you*?"

Along with those prayers, be sure to spend time in prayer thanking God for the husband or wife He has given you. Thank Him for making him or her unique and surprising.

Make a list of the ways your spouse continually surprises you. Find a way this week to show your spouse how much you love that unique aspect of his or her personality.

WEEK 3

WHATEVER
·········
IT TAKES

CONNECT

● **START YOUR GROUP TIME** by discussing what participants discovered in their Reflect homework.

Answer the following questions with your group. Be aware that some of your conversations may bring up painful memories and not every group member will have an answer for the questions below. Be sensitive to participants who may be reluctant to share.

What is your favorite childhood memory?

Were there any times in your childhood, or teenage years, where your parents did "whatever it takes" to show you love? Describe one of those instances.

What role did your parents play in your walk with Christ?

How has your own parents' faith affected the way you disciple your children?

Wanting to Believe

WATCH

- **WATCH CLIP 3** from the study DVD and answer the following questions:

    Have you ever felt pursued by someone? What did they do to pursue you?

    What does it look like to pursue your husband or wife? To pursue your kids?

    Would your kids say you pursue your spouse? Would they say you pursue them? Why or why not?

Our kids know what we believe based on how we pursue them. They also pay attention to how we handle our own mistakes.

    Do your kids know you mess up? How can you teach them through your mistakes?

This week we will look at how our beliefs are displayed in parenting, as well as how to do whatever it takes to make sure our children believe in God's truth themselves.

Whatever It Takes

ENGAGE

● **CONTINUE YOUR GROUP TIME** with this discussion guide.

One of the most important ways we are called to live out what we believe is in our parenting. Our children listen to what we say we believe and watch to see if we live it out. They, more than anyone other than our spouse, will know if we are not living out our beliefs.

● **READ** Ephesians 6:1-4.

> What do these verses say the role of the child is?

> What is the role of the parent?

> How are you training and instructing your children in the Lord? How can you improve?

Children are called to obey their parents. They are to do as we say, but the caveat is that we, as parents, are instructing them in the way of the Lord, instructing them in line with what we believe and the truth of God's Word.

● **READ** Deuteronomy 6:4-9.

> What words should be in our hearts, that we're repeating to our children?

Make a list of the times and ways these verses say to repeat our beliefs to our children.

Make a list of very specific ways, times, and places you can express your beliefs to your children.

Way	Time	Place

Make plans this week to begin this practice of telling your kids what you believe and what Scripture says. It may be awkward at first, but it is important.

Write down at least three specific times and ways you will talk to your children about who God is in this next week. Let your spouse, your friend, or your small group leader know your plan so they can hold you accountable to it.

Passing your beliefs to your children is something I am passionate about not only because that is what God calls us to do, but also because it's what my mom and dad did.

My parents were determined to teach me the truth of the Bible. They parented with one key thing in mind: *what did I make of the truth?* They both were determined to know truth for themselves, to enjoy living in light of that truth, and then to expose me to that bright light.

● **READ** Proverbs 22:6.

What is the goal of parenting according to this verse?

How have you seen that play out in your own life, or in the lives around you?

Proverbs is full of wisdom for parents. While this verse—and others like it—seem like promises, they are instead adages that direct us toward general principles. Generally, if we teach our children the way they should go, they will not depart from it. That's why the foundation of Scripture is important. However, we live in a fallen world and sometimes that means the proverbs are not a clear "do this and that will happen" formula. All that is not to say that we should be discouraged from trying to teach our children. Instead, we should be encouraged to keep telling them the truth of God's Word, demonstrating our beliefs, and asking God to speak to our children in a voice they can understand, so that they will not depart from those ways.

> ## THIS WEEK'S INSIGHTS
> • • •
> - Children are to obey their parents; parents are to train and instruct their children in the Lord.
> - We are to talk about our beliefs with our children. This will have a lasting impact on their lives and their own beliefs.
> - If we train our children in the way they should go while they are in our care, it is most likely that they will continue in faith in Christ as they grow and mature into men and women.

What is one key belief you want your children to learn from you?

How can you teach them that key belief this week?

WRAP UP
• • •

THIS WEEK, make this your prayer as you strive to teach your children your beliefs.

> Father, thank You for being our one true God. Thank You for the truths you have passed onto us from generation to generation about who You are and what You have done for us. Please guide us as we teach our children about You and Your love and works. Please help us as we train our children in Your ways and truth. Amen.

REFLECT

● **READ AND COMPLETE** the activities for this section before your next group time. For further insight, read chapters 7 and 8 in the book *Wanting to Believe*.

Parenting may cause us to cry out "help my unbelief" more often than "I do believe!" It is one of the most challenging, yet most rewarding experiences in life. We love our children with a love we didn't even know existed before we became parents and want the best for them and their future. We would do anything to care and protect them.

Our children need to know this about us—they need to know how much we treasure them and how much we love them. We want to do whatever it takes to make sure they know they are cared for, protected, and loved unconditionally.

> Do your children know you love them? Do they know they are protected and cared for? How have you communicated that to them?

> How can you do a better job of getting that message across to them?

My dad always made sure I knew I was loved and protected and cared for. He told me, but he also demonstrated his love. More than anything, my dad made sure I knew the truth about God.

I have wandered away from the truth, I have been rebellious a time or two (or a hundred), and I have made decisions my dad would not necessarily wish for me. However, he always spoke truth to me and made me feel loved. One way he made sure of this was that he made sure I knew who I was.

Knowing who I was made knowing what I believe easier. My dad knew I was different from him. I would make different decisions than he did.

That did not affect our relationship. He wasn't going to spend his parenting influence on hair color or tattoos or clothes; no, he would save it for the one important thing: that I know the truth.

My dad's ultimate goal was to know God's truth for himself, to live out his beliefs in that truth, and then to expose me to it. He then was committed to standing back and watching what I did with the truth—would it arrest me? Change me? Penetrate the tall walls I'd built?

This is the gift my dad gave me: he provided enough rope for me either to hang myself, or else to knot myself to an anchor that would weather every one of life's storms. Of course that anchor is Jesus, and wisely, I chose that route.

He demonstrated his beliefs for me. He knew the truth; he knew what he believed. And he invited me to believe, too.

● **READ** Deuteronomy 4:9.

> What did God tell the Israelites to teach their children?

> Think about your own walk with Christ. What have your eyes seen? How can you teach those things to your children?

One of the best ways to talk about Jesus and our beliefs with our children is by talking about what He has done and what He continues to do in our lives. Be open about your walk, your struggles, and your victories with your children.

● **READ** Titus 2:8.

> What does it mean to have dignity and integrity in your teaching? What does that look like in your home?

> Would your children say your message is beyond reproach? Why or why not?

The truth is that our children will learn from the life we live. Depending on how we demonstrate our walk with Christ, our children will either repeat the positive or negative patterns in our lives or learn from them. Don't shy away from telling your kids about your mistakes, but make sure they also see and know how to repent and change from watching you.

When what we believe is the most important thing to us, we want to make sure our children believe it, too. We want them to know the joy, the blessings, and the life available in Jesus. We want them to be our children and also our brothers and sisters in Christ.

It's easy to wonder and dream about the lives our children may someday lead. What will they do? Where will they go? Whom will they choose to be with? I praise God that my dad majored in the majors and kept the minors minor. I pray that I am the same way for my kids.

● **READ** Philippians 4:4-7.

> What do you tend to worry about when it comes to your children?

What do these verses say to do with that worry?

There should be balance in our parenting as we help our children feel loved and protected and also help them learn to trust God. Kids need to be lovingly, carefully trained up, in order to effectively navigate life. They need to be protected at all costs—to the ends of the earth, if you will. We shelter them when they are young so that we can help them soar later.

Conversely, we must not sinfully worry about our children. One of the keys to overcoming this is to go to God in prayer. We have to trust that He will work to conform His people to Jesus (see Rom. 8:28-29), including us and our children. Part of that trust is the call to petition God with our requests. We should pray for our children daily.

Desiring God Ministries provides a list of seven key things parents should pray for their children. Read through the list and the accompanying verses. Which items do you already pray for? Which do you need to start praying for?

1. That Jesus will call them and no one will hinder them from coming. (See Matt. 19:13-15.)
2. That they will respond in faith to Jesus' faithful, persistent call. (See 2 Pet. 3:9.)
3. That they will experience sanctification through the transforming work of the Holy Spirit and will increasingly desire to fulfill the greatest commandments. (See Matt. 22:37-39.)
4. That they will not be unequally yoked in intimate relationships, especially marriage. (See 2 Cor. 6:14.)
5. That their thoughts will be pure. (See Phil. 4:8.)
6. That their hearts will be stirred to give generously to the Lord's work. (See Ex. 35:29.)
7. That when the time is right, they will go. (See Matt. 28:18-20.)[1]

REFLECT

Are there any prayers you would add to the list? Consider rounding out the list to ten items. Be sure to attach each item to a verse or passage from the Bible.

PERSONAL REFLECTION
• • •

When you and I become moms and dads, we become stewards of another person's soul. We are that kid's primary shot at growing up safe and strong and spiritually pointed toward God—a huge task, to be sure. We are to train up our children in the truth, both telling and demonstrating what we believe.

What areas of parenting do you excel in?

What areas could use some work?

What steps are you taking this week to show your kids what you believe, in order that they might know and believe the truth?

---

1. Jon Bloom, "Seven Things to Pray for Your Children," *Desiring God* (online), 8 March 2013 [cited 19 June 2014]. Available from the Internet: *www.desiringGod.org*.

Wanting to Believe

WEEK 4
REMEMBER THE
INDIVIDUAL

CONNECT

● **START YOUR GROUP TIME** by discussing what participants discovered in their Reflect homework.

When we treat our spouses and children in line with our beliefs—the way God outlines in His Word to treat them—others will notice. However, we can't stop living out our beliefs with our family members. We must also remember to love those around us—our neighbors, friends, coworkers, and acquaintances.

> What is the nicest thing a friend has ever done for you?

> What is the nicest thing a stranger has done for you? Or that you witnessed a stranger doing for someone else?

> How have you been treated without respect? What did that feel like?

> On the other hand, how have you been treated kindly, perhaps at a time when it didn't make sense? What was that like?

Wanting to Believe

WATCH

● **WATCH CLIP 4** from the study DVD and answer the following questions:

Describe a time when you've seen the power of prayer displayed in your life.

How do you pray for your spouse? For your kids? For others around you?

Make a prayer plan. Write down things to pray for each day of the week. Set aside the time on your schedule to pray alone, with your spouse, and with your kids. Pray through each of the requests.

When we think about living out our beliefs about who God is and what He does for us, we think of prayer. Prayer is one of the ways we communicate with God to learn more about Him, and therefore, what we believe. Prayer for ourselves as well as others is one of the most powerful ways we can live out what we believe.

Take prayer requests as a group. Spend some time praying over them before moving on to the Engage section of the study.

Remember the Individual

ENGAGE

● **CONTINUE YOUR GROUP TIME** with this discussion guide.

When we know and believe who God is and what He's done and continues to do for us, it affects not only our marriage and our parenting, but how we interact with everyone around us. We must not only believe, but obey. That includes the commands God has given for us to remember the individual and love them as ourselves.

● **READ** Matthew 22:34-40.

You're probably familiar with this passage. It's quoted by Christians and non-Christians alike. Don't let familiarity affect its impact.

> How are we to love God?

> What does it look like to love God with all our heart, all our soul, and all our mind?

> How are we to love others?

> What does it look like practically to love someone as you love yourself?

We are inherently selfish people. We love ourselves, even if we don't always like ourselves. We want what is best for us, or at least what we've determined is best. We strive to get those things, no matter the cost. As long as it doesn't cost *us* too much. We want others to love us as much as we love ourselves.

Wanting to Believe

Jesus is asking us to do something that is the opposite of our nature. He is asking us to love others, to seek out the good of others, to try to help others, to build one another up.

● **READ** Exodus 20:1-17.

> Which commandments teach us how to love God with our hearts, souls, and minds?

> Which commandments teach us how to love others?

Jesus said that all the Law and Prophets boil down to loving God and loving others. The Ten Commandments show us how to do that. We often think of them as a list of don'ts, but they are essentially teaching us how to love God with our whole being and how to treat others like we'd want to be treated.

● **READ** Romans 12:9-21.

> According to this passage, how should believers treat those around them?

> How would it look in your life to "outdo" others in showing honor?

> Whom do you know who lives out these directives well?

Remember the Individual

When we believe, it will change the way we treat those around us. Our lives will begin to look more like Romans 12 every day. That's what it means to know and believe and to live out those beliefs with those around us.

I'm very grateful that I've seen these attributes lived out in my dad. As someone who has ministered to thousands of people over the years, my dad has done his best to love individuals like Romans 12.

He has always been concerned with remembering the individual. Because the individual matters.

> Is there a person—or perhaps a company or organization—you know who is great at remembering the individual? Give an example of how they do that.

> Think of people you normally fail to see as an individual needing love. How can you see them differently this week?

THIS WEEK'S INSIGHTS
• • •

- We are to love others as much as we love ourselves.
- The commandments are written so that we can know how to love God and love others. They show us how.
- We should try to outdo one another with love—rejoicing when those around us rejoice and weeping when they weep.
- Remember the individual. The individual matters.

What is your biggest obstacle in loving others?

Name one thing you can do today to love someone as you love yourself.

WRAP UP
• • •

THIS WEEK, pray that you will see the people around you as individuals in need of love.

> Jesus, thank You for loving me. Thank You for loving us each individually. Thank You for being the ultimate example of how to treat those around me. Please help me to follow in Your example and love those around me. Amen.

Remember the Individual

REFLECT

- **READ AND COMPLETE** the activities for this section before your next group time. For further insight, read chapters 10, 12, 13, and 15 in the book *Wanting to Believe*.

Practicing what we believe means that we treat people as individuals, loving them as we love ourselves. Living out our beliefs in relationship isn't easy. It means our behaviors will change, but it also means our words will be different.

- **READ** Psalm 69:6.

> Have you ever seen someone be disgraced or humiliated, like this verse talks about?

> Put this verse in your own words, making it your prayer as you think this week about how you interact with those around you.

This verse was my dad's prayer. He prayed that nothing he would ever do or say would bring any shame upon the Lord or His people. This prayer has affected the way he has interacted with thousands of people throughout the years. His desire is to be careful, thoughtful, measured, sure.

WORDS HAVE POWER

A huge part of the way we interact with others has to do with our words. People know what we believe by what we tell them. They know what we believe by the way we talk to our spouses, our children, and each other.

● **READ** James 3:3-6.

> Why do you think James compared the tongue to a horse's bit and a ship's rudder?

> What does that tell us about our words and how we use them?

Our words are incredibly powerful. What we say can impact the lives around us for Jesus or against Him. Words always are creative; with them we create goodness, or else we create what's bad.

The tongue is like the single spark that starts a wildfire. We can use it to praise God, but we can also use it to curse those we claim to love. The challenge, then, is to learn to restrain our tongue's natural inclinations. Otherwise, we set fire to our relational world.

My dad has attempted to be a man of restraint. He isn't perfect, but he always strives to be careful. We'll never be perfect with our words, but we can be careful with them. We can try to always create goodness with what we say.

● **READ** Matthew 12:33-37.

> What controls our words, according to these verses?

> Do you notice a difference in your words in seasons when you spend more or less time with God and in His Word?

> Would others know what you believe by your words?

These verses are sobering. To hear that one day we'll have to give account for every careless word we've said is not necessarily encouraging. But Jesus also says that it is by our words we'll be acquitted and by them we'll be condemned. This is why words matter. Our words are who we are.

YOUR YES HAS GOT TO BE YOUR YES

Because our words matter, we have to be careful with the words we choose and with what we say we'll do. When we are living like we believe in Jesus, we're treating others as we would like to be treated. I don't know about you, but I like to be told the truth.

● **READ** Matthew 5:33-37.

> Do you tend to let your yes be yes and your no be no? How would your spouse answer that question about you? Your kids? Your friends, coworkers, neighbors?

These verses are nestled in between exhortations on things like divorce and adultery and murder. They are part of the Sermon on the Mount, one of Jesus' most familiar teachings.

> What does the placement of these verses tell us about their importance? Why do you think it is important for us to keep our word?

Wanting to Believe

A lot of the Sermon on the Mount reads like a how-to guide for living like followers of Christ. Be gentle, don't hate, this is how you pray, give generously. In this same sermon, Jesus inserts, "Tell the truth." His followers should do what we say we will. We should be people of our word.

We may not often "swear oaths," but we have our own version. We say, "I promise" or "you have my word." Jesus comes into this and just says, "Hey, how about we don't swear? What if we just did what we said we'd do?" In a culture that shies away from commitment of any kind, this behavior is notable. Can you imagine what might happen in our world if we all lived by our word? Can you imagine the impact you'd have on those around you if you lived by your word?

RESULTS SHOW INTENTIONS

My wife once worked for a man who told his employees repeatedly, "Results show intentions." We can know and believe in God's truth all day, but our lives must show it. Our intentions are measured by the results. We can believe, but the world won't know it until they see the results of our belief.

● **READ** Psalm 15.

> What are the qualifications for someone who can dwell in the Lord's tent?

> What do these qualifications say about what the person believes?

> Do you do any of these things well? Are there any you need to work on?

Remember the Individual   55

Our beliefs determine how we treat others. If we believe in the truth of who Jesus is, we will be people of our word, we will speak carefully, and the results of the way we live will show our intentions of pleasing Him.

PERSONAL REFLECTION
• • •

As we finish this study, I hope you are more able to cry out to Jesus, "I do believe!" Not only do I pray you believe, but I pray you live out those beliefs in your relationships. I pray your spouse, your children, and those with whom you interact will know you are a follower of Jesus, that you believe.

How do you need to change the way you speak to more accurately reflect your beliefs?

....
....
....
....
....

If results show intentions, what would those around you say your intentions are? What steps can you take to make their answers align with your beliefs, if they don't already?

....
....
....
....
....
....

Key Insights

WEEK 1
- Believing in God's promises takes faith. Sometimes we have to ask for help when we struggle with unbelief.
- It is important to know what we believe.
- Our beliefs will affect our behavior.

WEEK 2
- One of the best ways to live out our beliefs is through a happy and committed marriage.
- Love is a choice. Because of Jesus, we can choose to love at every opportunity.
- We must put off frustration and put on fascination when it comes to our spouses and our differences.

WEEK 3
- Children are to obey their parents; parents are to train and instruct their children in the Lord.
- We are to talk about our beliefs with our children. This will have a lasting impact on their lives and their own beliefs.
- If we train our children in the way they should go while they are in our care, it is most likely that they will continue in faith in Christ as they grow and mature into men and women.

WEEK 4
- We are to love others as much as we love ourselves.
- The commandments are written so that we can know how to love God and love others. They show us how.
- We should try to outdo one another with love—rejoicing when those around us rejoice and weeping when they weep.
- Remember the individual. The individual matters.

Leader Notes

It's time for a leadership adventure. Don't worry; you don't have to have all the answers. Your role is to facilitate the group discussion, getting participants back on topic when they stray, encouraging everyone to share honestly and authentically, and guiding those who might dominate the conversation to make sure others are also getting some time to share.

As facilitator, take time to look over this entire study guide, noting the order and requirements of each session. Watch all the videos as well. Take time to read the suggested chapters (noted in the beginning of each Reflect section) from the book *Wanting to Believe* (ISBN 978-1-4336-8252-0). And pray over the material, the prospective participants, and your time together.

You have the option of extending your group's study by showing the films *Wanting to Believe* and *Your Legacy*. You can also keep it to four weeks by using just this study guide and DVD. The study is easy to customize for your group's needs.

Go over the How to Use This Study and the Guidelines for Groups sections with participants, making everyone aware of best practices and the steps of each session. Then dive into Week 1.

In establishing a schedule for each group meeting, consider ordering these elements for the hour of time together:

1. Connect—10 minutes
2. Watch—15 minutes
3. Engage—35 minutes

Be sure to allow time during each session to show the video clip. All four clips are approximately eight minutes or less in length. Reflect refers to the home study or activities done between group sessions.

Beginning with session 2, encourage some sharing regarding the previous week's Reflect home study. Usually at least one Connect question allows for this interaction. Sharing about the previous week's activities encourages participants to study on their own and be ready to share with their group during the next session.

As the study comes to a close, consider some ways to keep in touch. There may be some additional studies for which group members would like information. Some may be interested in knowing more about your church.

Occasionally, a group member may have needs that fall outside the realm of a supportive small group. If someone would be better served by the pastoral staff at your church or a professional counselor, please maintain a list of professionals to privately offer to that person, placing his/her road to recovery in the hands of a qualified pastor or counselor.

Use the space below to make notes or to identify specific page numbers and questions you would like to discuss with your small group each week based on their needs and season of life.

Further Resources

Need more guidance? Check out the following for help.

ON MARRIAGE:
Love for a Lifetime by Dr. James Dobson
What the Bible Says About Love, Marriage, and Sex by David Jeremiah
Experiencing God at Home by Richard Blackaby and Tom Blackaby
The Resolution for Men by Randy Alcorn, Stephen Kendrick, and Alex Kendrick
The Resolution for Women by Priscilla Shirer
Men Are Like Waffles, Women Are Like Spaghetti: Understanding and Delighting in Your Differences by Bill and Pam Farrel
Extraordinary Marriage: God's Plan for Your Journey by Rodney and Selma Wilson

ON PARENTING:
The New Dare to Discipline by Dr. James Dobson
The New Strong-Willed Child by Dr. James Dobson
Bringing Up Boys by Dr. James Dobson
Bringing Up Girls by Dr. James Dobson
Dr. Dobson's Handbook of Family Advice by Dr. James Dobson
Raising Boys and Girls by Sissy Goff, David Thomas, and Melissa Trevathan
Love No Matter What by Brenda Garrison
Intentional Parenting by Sissy Goff, David Thomas, and Melissa Trevathan
Raising Girls by Melissa Trevathan and Sissy Goff
The Back Door to Your Teen's Heart by Melissa Trevathan
5 Conversations You Must Have with Your Daughter by Vicki Courtney
Parenting Teens magazine
HomeLife magazine
ParentLife magazine
The Parent Adventure by Selma and Rodney Wilson
Experiencing God at Home by Richard Blackaby and Tom Blackaby
Authentic Parenting in a Postmodern Culture by Mary E. DeMuth
Grace-Based Parenting by Tim Kimmel

Introducing Your Child to Christ

Your most significant calling and privilege as a parent is to introduce your children to Jesus Christ. A good way to begin this conversation is to tell them about your own faith journey.

Outlined below is a simple gospel presentation you can share with your child. Define any terms they don't understand and make it more conversational, letting the Spirit guide your words and allowing your child to ask questions and contribute along the way.

GOD RULES. The Bible tells us God created everything, and He's in charge of everything. (See Gen. 1:1; Col. 1:16-17; Rev. 4:11.)

WE SINNED. We all choose to disobey God. The Bible calls this sin. Sin separates us from God and deserves God's punishment of death. (See Rom. 3:23; 6:23.)

GOD PROVIDED. God sent Jesus, the perfect solution to our sin problem, to rescue us from the punishment we deserve. It's something we, as sinners, could never earn on our own. Jesus alone saves us. (See John 3:16; Eph. 2:8-9.)

JESUS GIVES. He lived a perfect life, died on the cross for our sins, and rose again. Because Jesus gave up His life for us, we can be welcomed into God's family for eternity. This is the best gift ever! (See Rom. 5:8; 2 Cor. 5:21; Eph. 2:8-9; 1 Pet. 3:18.)

WE RESPOND. Believe in your heart that Jesus alone saves you through what He's already done on the cross. Repent, by turning away from your sin. Tell God and others that your faith is in Jesus. (See John 14:6; Rom. 10:9-10,13.)

If your child is ready to respond, explain what it means for Jesus to be Lord of his or her life. Guide your child to a time in prayer to repent and express his or her belief in Jesus. If your child responds in faith, celebrate! You now have the opportunity to disciple your child to be more like Christ.

BUILD YOUR FAMILY LEGACY.

Dr. James Dobson leads you through his classic messages and new insights for today's families in these eight DVD-based Bible studies. Each Building a Family Legacy Bible study includes four-sessions with personal reflection and discussion guides along with a DVD of Dr. Dobson's teachings, introduced by his son, Ryan. Studies include:

Your Legacy Bible Study
Bringing Up Boys Bible Study
Bringing Up Girls Bible Study
Dare to Discipline Bible Study
The Strong-Willed Child Bible Study
Straight Talk to Men Bible Study
Love for a Lifetime Bible Study
Wanting to Believe Bible Study

Learn more at LifeWay.com/Legacy

LifeWay
Biblical Solutions for Life